# mod_perl
*Pocket Reference*

# mod_perl
*Pocket Reference*

Andrew Ford

Beijing • Cambridge • Farnham • Köln • Paris • Sebastopol • Taipei • Tokyo

# mod_perl Pocket Reference

by Andrew Ford

Copyright © 2001 Ford & Mason Ltd. All rights reserved.
Printed in the United States of America.

Published by O'Reilly & Associates, Inc., 101 Morris Street,
Sebastopol, CA 95472.

**Editors:** Paula Ferguson and Gigi Estabrook

**Production Editor:** Emily Quill

**Cover Designer:** Ellie Volckhausen

**Printing History:**

January 2001:        First Edition.

Library of Congress Cataloging-in-Publication data can be found at:

*http://www.oreilly.com/catalog/modperlpr/*

0-596-00047-2                                                   4/01
[C]

# Table of Contents

# mod_perl Pocket Reference

## Introduction

Apache is the world's most popular web server, and Perl is the most popular server-side web scripting language. *mod_perl*, an Apache module created by Doug MacEachern, brings the two together, embedding a complete Perl interpreter into Apache and providing comprehensive Perl access to the Apache API, which it presents as a set of Perl classes.

*mod_perl* provides facilities to run Perl CGI scripts (either unaltered or with only minor changes) within the Apache server process, which allows Perl to be used in Server-Side Includes, and to write content handlers and handlers for other request processing phases in Perl. The Perl code is normally loaded and compiled at server startup or on the first request that requires it; either case results in significantly faster response time and lower server loading than the standard CGI model.

This pocket reference summarizes the *mod_perl* API and configuration directives, covering *mod_perl* Version 1.24. Not all functionality described here is necessarily enabled in any specific installation of *mod_perl*—it depends on how that copy of *mod_perl* was built. Neither is this book a self-contained user guide—it presupposes familiarity with *mod_perl*, general knowledge of web server technology, and an understanding of object-oriented Perl programming. For more information on *mod_perl*, see the Apache/Perl Integration Project web site at *http://perl.apache.org*.

# Acknowledgments

Heartfelt thanks to everyone who helped me so generously with this book, especially Stas Bekman, Gigi Estabrook, Paula Ferguson, Doug MacEachern, Catherine Mason, Lenny Muellner, Honza Pazdziora, Emily Quill, and Geoffrey Young. Thanks also to the other technical reviewers, too numerous to list, whose contributions eliminated many errors. For any that remain, I claim full credit.

# Typographic Conventions

This book uses the following formatting conventions:

*italic*
> Used for filenames, directories, class names, URIs, and URLs

constant width
> Denotes literal text, such as variables, directives, and module names

*constant width italic*
> Denotes parameters that should be replaced with specific values

{A|B}
> Denotes alternatives

[text]
> Denotes optional text

... Indicates that the previous element may be repeated

# What Is mod_perl?

*mod_perl* is an Apache extension module that embeds a Perl interpreter within the Apache web server. By itself, Apache provides an API that allows most aspects of request processing to be customized. *mod_perl* consists of C glue code that encapsulates the Perl runtime library and presents an interface to the Apache API as a set of Perl classes, allowing Apache modules to be written entirely in Perl.

Executing Perl code within the server process avoids much of the overhead normally associated with running Perl CGI scripts, such as starting a separate process, loading and initializing the Perl interpreter, and loading the Perl script and any Perl modules it references.

## The HTTP Protocol

HTTP—the Hypertext Transfer Protocol—is the foundation upon which the web is built. Web servers accept HTTP requests and reply with HTTP responses. *mod_perl* applications are effectively part of the web server, so creating them requires a good understanding of the HTTP protocol. For example, it is the programmer's responsibility to ensure that generated responses contain valid headers. A list of HTTP headers and status codes is provided later in this book; more detail can be found in Clinton Wong's *HTTP Pocket Reference* (O'Reilly).

## Processes, Requests, and Subrequests

On Unix-type systems, Apache uses a pre-forking process model. The main Apache process reads the configuration file and starts a number of child processes to handle incoming requests. The main process then monitors the child processes, starting new processes and killing superfluous idle processes, to maintain a pool of processes that are ready to accept new connections.

Apache handles requests in a number of phases. Modules register handlers for the specific phases they need to influence; most modules register handlers for only one or two phases. Apache calls each handler registered for a particular phase in turn, until all handlers have been called or until a handler indicates either that processing of the phase is complete or

---

that an error has occurred. The following table lists the phases in the order in which they occur.

| Phase | Purpose |
|-------|---------|
| Child initialization | Performs any necessary initialization when a child process is started (not called for every request). |
| Post-read request | Initial phase after the request headers have been parsed. |
| URI translation | Translates the URI into the filesystem namespace. |
| Header parsing | First phase in which <Directory> sections can be used (since the post-read request phase was introduced, this phase is no longer used by any standard Apache modules). |
| Access control | Applies access controls not based on user credentials. |
| Authentication | Checks the user's credentials. |
| Authorization | Checks whether the authenticated user is allowed to access the resource. |
| MIME type checking | Determines the attributes of the resource, such as document content type. |
| Fix-up | Makes any adjustments before the content generation phase. |
| Content generation | Generates the response. |
| Request logging | Logs the request. |
| Cleanup | Performs any necessary cleanup once the request has been processed. |
| Child exit | Called just before the child process exits (not called for every request). |

This picture is complicated slightly in that modules can issue subrequests to return a document other than the one requested, or to check what the response would be if a request were made for a different resource. Subrequests are processed starting at the the URI translation phase and stopping before the content generation phase.

## Sources of Further Information

The following sources contain further information on *mod_perl* and related topics.

### mod_perl

The Apache/Perl Integration Project web site (located at *http://perl.apache.org*) contains source code, documentation, the Apache/Perl Module List, and Stas Bekman's *mod_perl Guide*.

*Writing Apache Modules with Perl and C*, by Lincoln Stein and Doug MacEachern (O'Reilly).

### Apache

*Apache: The Definitive Guide*, by Ben Laurie and Peter Laurie (O'Reilly).

*Professional Apache*, by Peter Wainwright (Wrox Press).

*Apache Pocket Reference*, by Andrew Ford (O'Reilly).

*HTTP Pocket Reference*, by Clinton Wong (O'Reilly).

### Object-oriented Perl

*Programming Perl*, by Larry Wall, Tom Christiansen, and Jon Orwant (O'Reilly).

*Object Oriented Perl*, by Damien Conway (Manning).

*Advanced Perl Programming*, by Sriram Srinivasan (O'Reilly).

*CGI Programming with Perl*, by Scott Guelich, Shishir Gundavaram, and Gunther Birznieks (O'Reilly).

## Setting Up mod_perl

To use *mod_perl*, you must have Apache, Perl, and the *mod_perl* module installed. The simplest way to do this is to get a precompiled binary package. *mod_perl* has many compile-time options, however, and if the package you install was not built with the options you need, you will probably end up building it yourself anyway. Instructions for building *mod_perl* can be found in the source distribution, and also in *Writing Apache Modules with Perl and C* and the *mod_perl Guide*.

## Configuring Apache for mod_perl

Once *mod_perl* is installed, Apache must be configured to use it for particular requests. Apache is configured with directives specified in one or more configuration files, and *mod_perl* adds a number of directives to the standard complement.

The first step is to ensure that the *mod_perl* module is loaded into Apache and is active. If *mod_perl* was built as a loadable module (called a *Dynamic Shared Object* or DSO in the Apache documentation), you need to add the following line to the server configuration file:

```
LoadModule libexec/libperl.so
```

This is not needed if *mod_perl* is statically linked with Apache, however.

The default behavior of the configuration files distributed with Apache is to clear the internal list of active modules and then rebuild it in a particular order. If this is the case in your configuration files, you need to ensure that the following directive is present, or *mod_perl* will not be activated:

```
AddModule mod_perl.c
```

The simplest use of *mod_perl* is to configure a Perl handler for the content generation phase. For this to work, Apache must be told that *mod_perl* is the Apache module handling this phase, and *mod_perl* must be told which Perl handler function to invoke. For example:

```
<IfModule mod_perl.c>
    <Location /perl-bin>
        SetHandler  perl-script
        PerlHandler Apache::Registry
    </Location>
</IfModule>
```

This example wraps the directives in an <IfModule> block, which ensures that if *mod_perl* is not active, Apache will ignore the directives, instead of complaining about invalid directives and exiting.

*mod_perl* also allows you to configure Apache dynamically by enclosing Perl code in <Perl> sections in the server configuration files.

## Loading Perl Code

The `PerlModule` and `PerlRequire` directives load Perl code into the interpreter running within Apache at server startup. `PerlModule` loads one or more modules, while `PerlRequire` loads specified scripts. A common strategy is to specify a startup script with `PerlRequire`:

```
<IfModule mod_perl.c>
    PerlRequire /web/scripts/load-modules.pl
</IfModule>
```

and then load all required modules from that script:

```
#!/usr/bin/perl
# script to load modules at Apache start-up
use Apache::Registry ();
use CGI ();
# etc, etc
1;
```

Perl code can also be included directly in the server configuration files, enclosed in <Perl> sections.

Every module included with `use()` should be given an explicit import list, as each imported symbol takes up memory and accepting a module's default export list consumes memory unnecessarily.

The memory used by the Perl code and associated variables loaded at startup is normally shared between the main Apache process and all child server processes. On an operating system that utilizes "copy-on-write" memory management, however, each child process gets its own copy of any memory

---

pages that are modified, either by reloading modules or modifying variables, which increases the overall memory usage.

## Security Issues

Any script running on a web server is a potential security problem, but Perl code running under *mod_perl* has access to anything that Apache does. As Apache is normally started with root privileges, any code loaded with `PerlModule` or `PerlRequire` has access to the entire system. If you are responsible for running a web server, you should be careful about any code you write for *mod_perl* and positively paranoid about third-party code. You should also ensure that file permissions are set appropriately for all scripts, modules, and configuration files: none of these should be globally writable or writable by the user ID that Apache changes to when executing child server processes.

## Documenting Configuration Files

*mod_perl* recognizes a number of Perl's *pod* (plain old documentation) directives. This allows Apache configuration files to be documented with embedded pod directives and then reformatted as Unix manpages, HTML, PostScript, and so on, using the appropriate pod translator.

A pod documentation section starts with a `=pod` directive and continues until a `=cut` directive is encountered. The token `__END__` is taken by *mod_perl* to indicate the logical end of file.

Apache directives within pod sections can be both evaluated as directives and included in the formatted documentation by enclosing them within an `=over` directive that includes the word `apache` anywhere on the line and the next `=back` directive. Note that pod tools normally refill text within paragraphs, except for indented lines, so it may be best to indent all your Apache directives between these pod directives so that they appear verbatim. For example:

```
=pod

=head1 PERL SCRIPT DIRECTORY

This text is commentary on the following directives that
set up a I<perl-bin> directory:

=over to apache

  <Location /perl-bin>
      SetHandler  perl-script
      PerlHandler Apache::Registry
  </Location>

=back

And this is a final line of commentary.

=cut
```

# Migrating CGI Scripts to mod_perl

One important use of *mod_perl* is to speed up existing Perl
CGI scripts. If you have been running a web server for some
time, you may well have a collection of such scripts. Fortu-
nately, you may not need to rewrite these scripts to benefit
from the improved performance of *mod_perl*. Two standard
Apache/Perl modules, Apache::Registry and Apache::Perl-
Run, simulate a CGI environment and between them allow
most Perl CGI scripts to be run either unchanged or with only
minor changes. Apache::PerlRun can handle more problem-
atic scripts with fewer changes, but Apache::Registry is
generally preferred, as it offers greater performance improve-
ments.

## Apache::Registry

The Apache::Registry module compiles and runs CGI scripts
within the Apache process, caching the compiled code to
avoid the overhead of recompilation on subsequent requests.
A script is reloaded only if its modification time changes.

---

`Apache::Registry` performs the same checks as the Apache *mod_cgi* module: the `ExecCGI` option must be enabled, and the file containing the script must have the execute permission bit set (at least on Unix-type systems). Apache can be configured to use `Apache::Registry` to handle all files in a *perl-scripts* directory as follows:

```
Alias    /perl-scripts/  /web/perl-scripts/

<Location /perl-scripts>
    SetHandler     perl-script
    PerlHandler    Apache::Registry
    Options        +ExecCGI
    PerlSendHeader On
</Location>
```

A common alternative configuration is to treat all *.pl* files as being handled by `Apache::Registry`:

```
<FilesMatch "\.pl$">
    SetHandler     perl-script
    PerlHandler    Apache::Registry
    Options        +ExecCGI
    PerlSendHeader On
</FilesMatch>
```

It is important to note that scripts run under *mod_perl* execute in a different environment than normal CGI scripts. A CGI script runs in a separate process from the web server, and the resources it uses are generally released when the script exits. A script run under *mod_perl*, on the other hand, may be executed repeatedly in any of the child processes, and state may be carried over from previous runs in a specific process. As such, you should not rely on variables being uninitialized at the start of a script, and you should explicitly perform any necessary cleanup actions such as closing files, releasing locks, and destroying large data structures. Including a use strict statement can help to trap many potential problems. If the -w command-line switch is specified in the #! line, it is honored.

To compile a script, `Apache::Registry` wraps it in Perl code that defines a subroutine within a unique package, and evaluates the code with the Perl `eval` operator. This transformation of the code has three side effects:

* `__END__` and `__DATA__` tokens are not allowed in the script, as they would indicate a logical end of file before the subroutine block was complete. They can still be used in modules included by the script, however.

* Global variables in the script are no longer in the `main` package.

* Subroutines and `my()` variables declared outside any subroutine are wrapped in the enclosing subroutine. References to the variables within the script's subroutines become references to lexical variables in an outer subroutine. Because of the way Perl works, code in the outer and inner subroutines cannot share the same variable. A solution to this problem is to pass the variables as arguments to the inner subroutine or, alternatively, to use package global variables declared with the `use vars` pragma.

`Apache::Registry` loads a script into the child server process on the first request for the script. The `Apache::Registry-Loader` module allows scripts to be preloaded into the parent server, which speeds the first response and allows the code to be shared between child processes.

Scripts run from `Apache::Registry` are not restricted to the normal CGI environment. A script can obtain a reference to the request object with `Apache->request` (or with the `shift` operator, as a reference to the request object is passed to the generated subroutine that wraps the script's code) and can use any of the *mod_perl* classes. The script should output an HTTP `Content-Type` header to specify the MIME type of the resulting document, followed by an empty line and the document body. Headers can be printed explicitly or by using *mod_perl* or the `CGI` module.

---

## Apache::PerlRun

Like `Apache::Registry`, `Apache::PerlRun` evaluates a CGI script in a unique package, but it does not wrap the code in a subroutine or cache the compiled code. Once the script has run, the temporary namespace is cleared. `Apache::PerlRun` is slower than `Apache::Registry` on subsequent requests for a script served by a particular child process, but `Apache::Perl-Run` can run many scripts that will not run under `Apache::Registry`. With `Apache::PerlRun`, modules included by the script are loaded into the server and so are still cached.

If a particular script is causing problems even under `Apache::PerlRun`, you can try adding the following directive to the appropriate server configuration file:

```
PerlSetVar    PerlRunOnce  On
```

This causes the process executing a script under `Apache::PerlRun` to terminate once it has finished the request. The directive can be included in a container section or per-directory configuration file to limit its effect to particular scripts.

## Migration Strategy

A sensible migration strategy for a preexisting CGI script might be the following procedure:

1.  Before running a CGI script under *mod_perl*, ensure that the script has a `use strict` statement and has been run with Perl warnings enabled (and that all warnings are understood).

2.  Configure Apache to run the script under `Apache::Perl-Run`.

3.  Tidy up the script so it runs under `Apache::Registry`.

4.  Rewrite the script to make use of *mod_perl*.

5.  Rewrite the script as a *mod_perl* module.

Obviously, you need to take only the steps necessary to get the script to work. Bear in mind, though, that following additional steps may improve the script's performance; it is a matter of balancing the effort required against the value of any potential performance benefits.

# Embedding Perl in HTML Documents

Embedding scripting commands within HTML pages is a well-known approach for adding limited dynamic functionality to web pages without resorting to low-level programming. There are a number of systems that accomplish this, ranging from Server-Side Includes (SSI), to template systems, to dedicated language processors such as PHP. The earliest such system was Server-Side Includes, which, in combination with *mod_perl*, allows fragments of Perl code to be used within the SSI tags.

There are several template systems that are either based on *mod_perl* or can be used with *mod_perl*. Explaining how to use these systems is outside the scope of this book, but they are listed later in the "Apache/Perl Modules" section. The template systems differ in the features they offer, but they typically provide more sophisticated facilities than SSI, such as caching compiled pages, session management, and libraries of components.

## Perl Server-Side Includes

There are two alternative implementations of SSI that allow Perl code to be used. First, the standard *mod_include* Apache module has been extended to allow the use of Perl code if *mod_perl* is built with the `PERL_SSI` option enabled. The second implementation is provided by the `Apache::SSI` Apache/Perl module, which can also be subclassed to add custom directives.

---

Both systems add a #perl directive, which allows you to invoke an arbitrary subroutine and have its output included in the web page, but there are subtle differences between the two. In both cases, the directive takes a sub attribute, which specifies the subroutine to be called, and an arg attribute, which specifies arguments to be passed to the subroutine (and which can occur multiple times). The Apache::SSI module also takes an args attribute specifying multiple comma-separated arguments. SSI attribute values must be quoted if they contain spaces, and quote characters within the strings must be escaped, either with a backslash or by using Perl's quoting operators.

The subroutine can be either a named subroutine that has already been loaded into the server or an anonymous subroutine. The subroutine is passed a reference to the request object followed by a list of specified arguments.

Standard Perl SSI (*mod_include*) looks for strings sub and arg in attribute names, accepting variations such as subroutine, arg1, and args. It also allows CGI and SSI variables to be interpolated into the values of the arg attributes. Apache::SSI checks for exact matches for the attribute names and does not interpolate CGI and SSI variables into attribute values.

This example illustrates the use of both an anonymous subroutine and escaped quotes in the value of the sub attribute:

```
<!--#perl sub="sub { my($r, @args) = @_;
                print qq{The arguments were: },
                    join(\"; \", @args);
            }"
        arg="First argument"
        args="$SERVER_NAME,$PATH_INFO"  -->
```

This is a rather contrived example in that it simply outputs the arguments passed to the subroutine, but it does demonstrate a number of concepts. Note that the second argument contains SSI variables. The example is valid under both extended *mod_include* and Apache::SSI, but standard SSI sees only two arguments (as it interprets args as synonymous with arg), while `Apache::SSI` splits the second argument in two and thus sees three arguments. The body of the anonymous subroutine also contains examples of escaped quotes and one of Perl's alternate quoting operators.

Perl SSI is available if the *mod_include* module is loaded. Note that the `Includes` option must be specified for directories that contain SSI files. Server-Side Includes can be configured as follows:

```
AddModule    mod_include.c
AddType      text/html       .shtml
SetHandler   server-parsed   .shtml
<Directory /web/htdocs>
    Options      +Includes
</Directory>
```

Under `Apache::SSI`, Server-Side Includes are handled by an Apache/Perl module, so they are set up with `SetHandler` and `PerlHandler` directives. The following example illustrates how to configure all *.phtml* files to be treated as Perl SSI:

```
<Files *.phtml>
    ForceType    text/html
    SetHandler   perl-script
    PerlHandler Apache::SSI
</Files>
```

## SSI Directives

*mod_include* implements the standard SSI directives listed here.

`<!--#config [attribute=value]... -->`

Configures aspects of parsing. Valid attributes are:

| Attribute | Significance |
|-----------|-------------|
| errmsg | Message returned if an error occurs during SSI parsing |
| sizefmt | Format to use for file sizes; either `bytes` or `abbrev` |
| timefmt | `strftime()` format string used for dates |

```
<!--#echo encoding={url|none} var=varname -->
```
Prints the value of a CGI or SSI variable specified with the var attribute.

```
<!--#set var=varname value=value -->
```
Sets the value of the specified variable.

```
<!--#printenv -->
```
Prints a list of all variables and their values.

```
<!--#exec {cmd=cmd-string|cgi=url-path} -->
```
Executes the specified shell command (using /bin/sh) or CGI script.

```
<!--#fsize {file=file-path|virtual=url-path} -->
```
Prints the size of the specified file.

```
<!--#flastmod {file=file-path|virtual=url-path} -->
```
Prints the last modification time of the specified file.

```
<!--#include {file=file-path|virtual=url-path} -->
```
Includes the specified file.

```
<!--#if expr="cond" -->
<!--#elif expr="cond" -->
<!--#else -->
<!--#endif -->
```
Define conditional blocks. The following comparison operators are supported: =, !=, <, <=, <, and >=. Comparisons can be enclosed in parentheses for grouping, prefixed by an exclamation point (!) to negate the condition, and combined with AND (&&) or OR (||) operators.

Perl SSI adds the following directive:

```
<!--#perl sub={subname|anon-sub}arg=value... -->
```
Invokes the named or anonymous Perl subroutine and includes its output.

# Programming mod_perl

While the most popular use of *mod_perl* is undoubtedly as a vehicle for running CGI scripts, its performance and flexibility are only fully realized in native *mod_perl* applications. Programming *mod_perl* applications is a huge topic and cannot be covered in detail here; consult the *mod_perl* sources listed earlier for more complete information. This section simply provides an overview of *mod_perl* programming. It covers the basics of handler functions for content generation and other phases, and offers guidance on debugging handlers, accessing configuration information and databases, and maintaining state between pages.

Writing a *mod_perl* application requires a different approach than writing a traditional CGI script, which is simply a standalone program invoked by the web server to handle the content generation phase. One important difference is that a *mod_perl* application can intervene in any or all of the request processing phases. Typically, however, a *mod_perl* application is focused on just one or two phases, and can be categorized by its main activity: generating content, imposing access restrictions, performing URI mapping, or determining a resource's MIME type. The Apache/Perl modules included in the *mod_perl* distribution (and on CPAN) provide a rich set of examples of what can be achieved with *mod_perl*.

## Handler Functions

A *mod_perl* application is structured as one or more callback handler functions configured to deal with particular request processing phases. A handler function is normally invoked with a single argument—a reference to a request object, conventionally named $r$—and is expected to return a status code that indicates the result of processing the phase for which it was invoked.

For each phase, Apache invokes each handler applicable to the request until a handler indicates that processing for that phase is complete. A handler should return the constant DECLINED if it decides not to process the phase, OK if the phase has been successfully processed, or an HTTP error code. If a handler returns DONE, request processing is terminated, and except when processing subrequests, Apache goes straight to the logging phase.

## Response handlers

The most common type of handler is a content handler, which generally has the following structure:

```
sub handler {
    my $r = shift;

    # Check that the MIME type is correct
    $r->content_type eq 'text/plain' || return DECLINED;

    # Send the HTTP headers, and output the content
    $r->send_http_header;
    $r->print("Hello world\n");

    # Return success to indicate the phase is complete
    return OK;
}
```

If the response to a particular URI changes infrequently, a handler should check for the presence of an IfModifiedSince HTTP header and, if possible, avoid resending the document. This can be achieved by setting the modification time and calling the meets_conditions() method. If the method returns anything other than OK, the handler simply returns with that value.

## Handlers for other phases

Handler functions can set attributes of the request using the methods described in the later section "The mod_perl API." The following list describes typical actions for handlers for particular phases:

*Translation*

The handler examines the URI and sets the translated file-name for requests being handled.

*Access control*

The handler examines aspects of the request, such as the remote IP address, the time of day, or the user agent, and returns FORBIDDEN if the request should be denied. For example:

```
sub handler {
    my $r = shift;
    return $r->remote_ip =~ /^10\./ ?
        DECLINED : FORBIDDEN;
}
```

*Authentication*

The handler returns AUTH_REQUIRED if the check fails and the handler's response is definitive, or DECLINED to defer the decision to the next authentication handler.

*MIME type checking*

The handler determines the MIME type and sets the content type, encoding, language, and other attributes.

*Logging*

The handler does whatever logging is needed. All log handlers applicable to a request are called, regardless of whether or not the request was processed successfully.

*Cleanup*

The handler cleans up after the application to avoid potential performance problems on subsequent requests. When a CGI script finishes processing a request, it exits and any resources it has acquired are released. In contrast, *mod_perl* applications run inside an Apache web server child process and stay resident even after the request has been served. Thus, resources acquired during request processing are not automatically released. Note that the HTTP transaction has been completed at this stage.

## Stacked handlers and method handlers

Handlers are normally installed for a particular phase with the Perl*Handler configuration directives. Multiple handlers can be specified with a single directive, and are invoked in the order specified. A handler can register other handlers for later phases with the push_handlers() method. The registered handlers are pushed on to the end of the handler stack and called after the handlers specified by configuration directives.

A handler can be defined with a prototype of ($$) to specify that it is a method handler. It is then configured as follows:

```
PerlHandler Apache::YourModule->handler
```

The method is invoked with a class name or blessed object as its first argument, and the blessed request object as its second argument. Method handlers allow inheritance of methods from other classes, but they cannot be used directly with push_handlers() because *mod_perl* invokes such functions with a single argument. This limitation can be circumvented by using a closure, however. For example:

```
sub fixup_handler ($$) {
    # ...
}

sub mime_type_handler ($$) {
    my($self, $r) = @_;

    $r->push_handlers(PerlFixupHandler =>
                    sub { my $r = shift;
                            $self->fixup_handler($r); } );
}
```

## Debugging mod_perl handlers

*mod_perl* handlers run in a complex environment that can be difficult to debug. It helps if the application has been modularized so that individual components can be unit-tested in isolation. The handler functions themselves can often be debugged with the help of the Apache::FakeRequest module, which sets up a dummy request object that can be passed to the handler. You can run a simple wrapper script like the following from the Perl debugger, enabling you to examine the behavior of your code:

```
#!/usr/bin/perl

use Apache::FakeRequest;
use Apache::YourModule;

my $r = Apache::FakeRequest->new(attr => value, ...);
Apache::YourModule::handler($r);
```

You can also debug Perl code while it is running under Apache with the Apache::DB modules, although the server has to be started with the -X command-line option in order to run it in single-process mode.

## Accessing Configuration Information

The ability to access runtime configuration information allows *mod_perl* applications to adapt to the particular requirements of individual web servers. Configuration information can be passed from the command line, the command environment, and Apache configuration files as values of elements of the %ENV hash and as values of per-directory variables specified by the PerlSetVar and PerlAddVar directives.

Apache normally sets up the environment for subprocesses prior to the content generation phase, copying the environment into elements of the %ENV hash. The PerlSetEnv and PerlPassEnv directives cause specified elements of the hash to be set up at the start of the request-processing cycle. Full initialization of the %ENV hash can be triggered at any point in the cycle by calling the subprocess_env() method in a void context without any arguments. The values of per-directory variables can be retrieved with the dir_config() method.

## Accessing Databases

Web applications often need to acccer and update information stored in SQL databases, but connecting and disconnecting for each request can impose an unacceptably high overhead. If the Apache::DBI module is loaded before the DBI module, database handles are cached and reused when the parameters on a subsequent connection request exactly match a previous connection. Connections made during server initialization in the main Apache process are not cached, however, and should be closed before child processes are started, as database handles cannot be shared between processes. Connections can be automatically opened in child processes using the connect_on_init() method.

In circumstances where database handles are unlikely to be reused, however, caching of the handles can be counterproductive. Apache::DBI overloads the disconnect() method as a no-op, so all database connections are kept open for the lifetime of each child process. On a busy server with applications that connect to the database using differing combinations of connection parameters, the load imposed by the caching of the connections could overwhelm the database server, as database servers allocate resources for connections. In such cases, it may be better not to use Apache::DBI.

## Maintaining State

Web applications that interact with users over a series of pages need to maintain state information. This information can be stored on the client side, in a hidden field of a form or in a cookie, or it can be embedded in a URI. Alternatively, the information can be stored on the server side in some form of database. In this case, only a unique session key needs to be passed back to the browser, since the key is sufficient for retrieving the necessary state information from the database. The Apache::Session module provides several ways of storing session state on the server.

# The mod_perl API

The *mod_perl* API is defined by a number of Perl classes that provide methods, special variables, and constants. In the descriptions of the methods in this section, the variables $s, $r, and $c are intended to represent a server object (Apache::Server), a request object (Apache), and a connection object (Apache::Connection), respectively.

All the features described here may not be available in a particular installation of *mod_perl*, depending on how that installation was built. You can use the mod_perl::hook() or Apache::perl_hook() method in your code to check whether a specific handler is supported.

Note that *mod_perl* provides many methods that either get or set the value of an attribute, depending on whether an optional argument is provided. When the optional argument is specified, such a method sets the value of the attribute and returns its previous value.

## The Request Object

Handlers are called with a reference to the current request object (Apache), which by convention is named $r.

$r = Apache >request([$r])

> Returns a reference to the request object. Perl handlers are called with a reference to the request object as the first argument.

$bool = $r->is_initial_req

> Returns true if the current request is the initial request, and false if it is a subrequest or an internal redirect.

$bool = $r->is_main

> Returns true if the current request is the initial request or an internal redirect, and false if it is a subrequest.

*$req = $r->last*
>    Returns a reference to the last request object in the chain. When used in a logging handler, this is the request object that generated the final result.

*$req = $r->main*
>    Returns a reference to the main (initial) request object, or undef if *$r* is the main request object.

*$req = $r->next*
>    Returns a reference to the next request object in the chain.

*$req = $r->prev*
>    Returns a reference to the previous request object in the chain. When used in an error handler, this is the request that triggered the error.

## The Apache::SubRequest Class

The Apache::SubRequest class is a subclass of Apache and inherits its methods.

*$subr = $r->lookup_file($filename)*
>    Fetches a subrequest object by filename.

*$subr = $r->lookup_uri($uri)*
>    Fetches a subrequest object by URI.

*$status = $subr->run*
>    Invokes the subrequest's content handler and returns the content handler's status code.

## Client Request Methods

This section covers methods for retrieving information about the current request.

*{$str|@array} = $r->args*
>    Returns the contents of the URI query string as a string in a scalar context or as a list of parsed key/value pairs in an array context. Note that assigning the list to a hash discards all but the last value for multi-valued keys.

---

*$c = $r*->connection

Returns a request connection object blessed into the Apache::Connection class.

*{$str|@array}* = *$r*->content

Returns the entity body read from the client as a string in a scalar context if the request content type was application/x-www-form-urlencoded. In a list context, a list of *name=value* pairs is returned. If the method is called more than once, it returns undef or an empty list on subsequent calls.

*$str* = *$r*->filename([*$newval*])

Returns the result of URI-to-filename translation. A handler can pass a string to the method to set the translated filename.

*$handle* = *$r*->finfo

Points the cached stat() info for the translated filename to the special filehandle Perl uses to cache its own stat() operations, and returns a reference to the handle.

*$str* = *$r*->get_remote_host([*$lookup_type*])

Looks up the client's DNS hostname. The :remotehost export tag of the Apache::Constants module provides the following symbolic names for the lookup type:

REMOTE_NAME

Returns the DNS name, if possible, or the IP address. This is the default lookup type.

REMOTE_HOST

Attempts to look up and return the DNS name. Returns undef if HostNameLookups is set to OFF or if the lookup fails.

REMOTE_NOLOOKUP

Returns the DNS name if it has already been looked up and cached, or the IP address otherwise.

REMOTE_DOUBLE_REV

> Triggers a double-reverse DNS lookup (looks up the hostname and then checks that the hostname maps back to the IP address of the remote host) and returns the DNS name or undef.

*$str* = *$r*->get_remote_logname

> Looks up and returns the client's identity on the remote system. Returns undef if the information cannot be obtained (if the remote system is not running an *ident* server or the IdentityCheck configuration directive is not set to ON). Note that performing identity checks causes delays and the information is often unavailable or unreliable, so it is best avoided (except possibly on an intranet).

{*$href|@array*} = *$r*->headers_in

> Returns the client request headers as a list of key/value pairs in an array context, or an Apache::Table object in a scalar context.

*$str* = *$r*->header_in(*$hdr*[, *$newval*])

> Gets or sets the value of the specified client request header. Removes the header if the new value is specified as undef.

*$bool* = *$r*->header_only

> Returns true if the client issued an HTTP HEAD request.

*$str* = *$r*->method([*$newval*])

> Gets or sets the request method as a string, such as "GET".

*$num* = *$r*->method_number([*$newval*])

> Gets or sets the request method number. The :methods export tag of the Apache::Constants class provides symbolic names for the methods.

*$u* = *$r*->parsed_uri

> Returns a reference to an Apache::URI object, which provides methods for getting and setting parts of the URI.

*$str* = *$r*->path_info([*$newval*])

> Gets or sets the additional path information component of the URI (what is left in the path after the URI translation phase).

*$str* = *$r*->protocol

> Returns a string identifying the protocol specified in the request, such as "HTTP/1.1".

*$bool* = *$r*->proxyreq([*$newval*])

> Gets or sets the value of a Boolean flag that indicates whether the current request is for a proxy URI.

*$r*->read(*$buf*, *$bytes_to_read*)

> Reads data submitted by the client in a POST or PUT request. A timeout is set internally prior to the read.

*$s* = *$r*->server

> Returns a reference to an Apache::Server object, which can be used to retrieve information about the server's configuration.

*$str* = *$r*->the_request

> Returns the raw request line sent by the client.

*$str* = *$r*->uri([*$newval*])

> Gets or sets the URI requested by the client.

## Server Response Methods

This section covers methods to construct and query the outgoing server response headers. Note that the response headers Content-Type, Content-Encoding, and Content-Language affect request handling behavior and should be set using the appropriate method, rather than the generic header_out method, or Apache may not recognize the changes.

*$num* = *$r*->bytes_sent

> Number of bytes of data sent to the client (useful only after the send_http_header() method has been called).

---

*$str* = *$r*->cgi_header_out(*$hdr*[, *$newval*])

> Gets the named outgoing HTTP header or sets it to the specified value. If the header has special meaning, the appropriate API functions are invoked to take the appropriate action.

*$str* = *$r*->content_encoding([*$newval*])

> Gets or sets the document content encoding.

*$aref* = *$r*->content_languages([*$newaref*])

> Gets or sets the content languages; the languages are specified by an array of two-letter language identifiers.

*$str* = *$r*->content_type([*$newval*])

> Gets or sets the document content type.

*$str* = *$r*->custom_response(*$code*[, *$response*])

> Gets or sets the custom response for a given status code. The response should be the message string to return or the URI to invoke if the specified error status is encountered. The URI may be that of a remote document, a script, or a static document. This is a hook into Apache's ErrorDocument mechanism.

{*$href*|*@array*} = *$r*->err_headers_out

> In a scalar context, returns a hash reference to the error headers table, tied to the Apache::Table class. In a list context, returns a list of key/value pairs that correspond to the error response headers.

*$str* = *$r*->err_header_out(*$hdr*[, *$newval*])

> Gets or sets a single field in the error headers table.

*$str* = *$r*->handler([*$newval*])

> Gets or sets the name of the handler responsible for content generation (as set by the AddHandler or SetHandler Apache directives).

{*$href*|*@array*} = *$r*->headers_out

> In a scalar context, returns a hash reference to the server response headers table, tied to the Apache::Table class. In a list context, returns a list of key/value pairs that correspond to the response headers.

---

*$str* = *$r*->header_out(*$hdr*[, *$newval*])

> Gets or sets a single field in the server response headers table.

*$bool* = *$r*->no_cache([*$newval*])

> Gets or sets a Boolean flag. If true, the flag causes Apache to generate headers to inform clients that the resource is not cachable (i.e., an Expires header with a value of the time of the original request, a Pragma: no-cache header, and a Cache-control: no-cache header).

*$num* = *$r*->request_time

> Returns the time at which the request started as a Unix time value.

*$num* = *$r*->status([*$newval*])

> Gets or sets the status code of the outgoing response. Symbolic names for all standard status codes are provided by the Apache::Constants module.

*$str* = *$r*->status_line([*$newval*])

> Gets or sets the status line that is sent to the client. This should include the numeric HTTP status code and a human-readable string.

## Sending Data to the Client

This section covers methods for sending header and document body data to the client. These methods may be used only during the content generation phase. The STDOUT filehandle is tied to the Apache class, so the built-in functions print() and printf() are redirected to the methods provided by that class.

*$r*->print(*@list*)

> Sends the values of the arguments to the client. If the $| variable is true, the stream is flushed after each command. If any of the arguments are references to scalar values, they are dereferenced and the values printed.

---

*$r*->printf(*$format*, *@args*)

> Sends a formatted string to the client.

*$r*->rflush

> Instructs Apache to flush any buffered output.

*$r*->send_cgi_header(*$str*)

> Parses the string into separate header lines, which are passed to the cgi_header_out() method, and then calls send_http_header(). The string should contain one header per line, terminated with a blank line.

*$len* = *$r*->send_fd(*$filehandle*)

> Sends the contents of the file open on the specified file-handle to the client.

*$r*->send_http_header([*$content_type*])

> Formats the outgoing headers into a proper HTTP response and sends them to the client. If a content type is specified as the optional argument, this overrides any previous setting.

## Server Core Functions

This section describes methods not directly related to I/O.

*$r*->chdir_file([*$filename*])

> Changes the current directory to the directory containing the specified file, or to the one containing *$r*->filename if no file is specified.

*$r*->child_terminate

> Instructs the child server process to terminate gracefully once the current request is complete (not available on Win32 systems).

*$r*->hard_timeout(*$msg*)

> Initiates a hard timeout. If the timeout occurs, Apache goes straight to the logging phase. Note that the use of this method is deprecated, as the timeout does not give the Perl interpreter a chance to clean up and may leave it in a confused state.

*$r*->internal_redirect(*$newplace*)

Stops processing the current request and starts a sub-request to return a different local URI instead. This method must be used only in a content handler. No result is returned, so the handler should return OK.

*$r*->internal_redirect_handler(*$newplace*)

Performs the same actions as the internal_redirect() method, but the content handler is the same as for the current request.

*$r*->kill_timeout

Cancels a previously initiated timeout.

*$str* = *$r*->location

Returns the location path if the current handler was invoked from a <Location> section.

{*$str*|*$href*} = *$r*->notes([*$key*[, *$newval*]])

Gets or sets an entry in the notes table, which is used for communication between modules. If called with no arguments in a scalar context, a reference to the notes table is returned. The key and new value, if specified, must be simple strings.

{*$str*|*$href*} = *$r*->pnotes([*$key*[, *$newval*]])

Gets or sets an entry in *mod_perl*'s pnotes per-request hash, which is used for communication between Perl modules. If called with no arguments in a scalar context, a reference to the notes table is returned. Unlike the notes() method, this method can take a reference as the scalar value.

*$r*->register_cleanup(*$code_ref*)

Registers a subroutine to be called after the request handling logging phase.

*$r*->reset_timeout

Resets the timeout timer back to zero.

`$r->soft_timeout($msg)`

> Initiates a "soft" timeout. If the timeout occurs, control returns to the handler, but all further read and write operations act as no-ops and the `Apache::Connection` `aborted()` method returns true.

`{$str|$href} = $r->subprocess_env([$key[, $newval]])`

> Gets or sets an entry in Apache's environment table. If called with no arguments in a scalar context, it returns a hash reference to the table, tied to the `Apache::Table` class. When called with no arguments in a void context, the table is reinitialized to contain the standard variables normally added before invoking CGI scripts.

## Server Configuration Methods

This section covers methods that give access to the Apache server configuration settings.

`$bool = $r->define($name)`

> Returns true if the named symbol was defined on the Apache command line with the `-D` switch.

`$str = $r->dir_config([$key])`

> Returns the value of a variable specified in one of the Apache configuration files with a `PerlSetVar` or `PerlAdd-Var` directive. When called in a scalar context with no arguments, it returns a hash reference tied to the `Apache::Table` class.

`$str = $r->document_root`

> Returns the name of the document root directory as set by the `DocumentRoot` directive.

`$str = $r->get_server_name`

> Returns the name of the server handling the request. This is the value of the current `ServerName` directive if `Use-CanonicalName` is `ON`; otherwise, it is the value of the request's `Host` header, if present.

---

*$num* = *$r*->get_server_port

Returns the port number of the server. If UseCanonical-Name is OFF and the client sent a Host header, this is the actual port on which the connection was received; otherwise, it is the value of the Port directive or the default port of 80 if no Port directive was used.

*$str* = *$r*->server_root_relative([*$path*])

Resolves a relative pathname to an absolute pathname based on the value specified by the ServerRoot directive. Without any arguments, the server root directory name is returned.

## Access Control Methods

This section covers methods for access control, authentication, and authorization.

*$opts* = *$r*->allow_options

Returns a bitmap of the options allowed in the current context. Symbolic constants are provided with the subroutines exported with the :options tag from the Apache::Constants class.

*$str* = *$r*->auth_name([*$newval*])

Gets or sets the current value of the authentication realm (configured with the AuthName configuration directive).

*$str* = *$r*->auth_type

Returns the authentication type (set with the AuthType configuration directive).

(*$rc*, *$pw*) = *$r*->get_basic_auth_pw

Returns a two-element list that contains the authentication status followed by the plain text password that the client supplied. The status element has the value OK if the current request is protected by basic authentication and authentication was successful; otherwise, it may have the value DECLINED, AUTH_REQUIRED, or SERVER_ERROR.

*$r*->note_basic_auth_failure

> Indicates to *mod_perl* that the client did not provide a valid username and password combination for a URI protected by basic authentication. *mod_perl* then sets up HTTP headers so that the user is challenged to provide this information.

*$aref* = *$r*->requires

> Returns a reference to an array of hash references, each of which contains two elements. The element with the key requirement is the argument of the Require directive, and the one with the key method_mask contains a bit mask indicating the HTTP methods that the requirements apply to. The :methods export tag of Apache::Constants class defines symbolic names for the bit values.

*$flag* = *$r*->satisfies

> Returns SATISFY_ALL, SATISFY_ANY, or SATISFY_NOSPEC, according to the setting of the Satisfy directive. These symbolic constants are defined by the :satisfy export tag of the Apache::Constants class.

*$bool* = *$r*->some_auth_required

> Returns true if the the current request requires some form of authentication or authorization.

## Logging and the Apache::Log Class

This section describes error logging methods. The first set of methods represents the error logging API prior to Apache 1.3.

*$str* = *$r*->as_string

> Formats the current client request and server response fields as a multi-line string. Used mainly for debugging.

*$r*->log_error(*$message*)

> Writes *$message* to the server error log, prefixed by a timestamp.

*$r*->log_reason(*$message*[, *$file*])

> Writes *$message* to the server error log, generating additional information that identifies the URI requested and the host from which the request originated. If *$file* is specified, that value is used in place of the URI.

*$r*->warn(*$message*)

> Writes *$message* to the server error log if the logging severity level (set with the LogLevel directive) is less than or equal to Warn.

Apache 1.3 introduced a set of eight log levels; the Apache::Log class provides methods to log a message at each of these levels. The message is written to the error log only if the severity level of the method is equal to or higher than that set with the LogLevel directive. Each method takes one or more strings or a reference to a subroutine that returns the string to be logged. The subroutine passed by reference is executed only if the log method determines that it should log the message, which avoids executing code to produce message strings that won't be used.

The Apache::Log class defines the following constants if *mod_perl* was built with Perl Version 5.6 or higher (but they are not exported by default): EMERG, ALERT, CRIT, ERR, WARNING, NOTICE, INFO, and DEBUG.

*$log* = *$r*->log

> Returns an object blessed into the Apache::Log class. Note that messages written with logging methods invoked on a log object obtained from a request object include the client's IP address, and the message is stored in the request's notes table under the key error-notes.

*$log* = *$s*->log

> Returns an object blessed into the Apache::Log class. Note that messages written with logging methods invoked on a log object obtained from a server object do not include the client's IP address.

---

*$log*->emerg({*$str*...|*$code_ref*})
> Logs an emergency-level message. This level normally indicates a condition that makes the server unusable.

*$log*->alert({*$str*...|*$code_ref*})
> Logs an alert-level message, indicating that immediate attention is required.

*$log*->crit({*$str*...|*$code_ref*})
> Logs a critical message, indicating a severe condition.

*$log*->error({*$str*...|*$code_ref*})
> Logs a noncritical error message.

*$log*->warn({*$str*...|*$code_ref*})
> Logs a warning that may or may not require attention.

*$log*->notice({*$str*...|*$code_ref*})
> Logs a notice of a normal but significant condition.

*$log*->info({*$str*...|*$code_ref*})
> Logs an informational message.

*$log*->debug({*$str*...|*$code_ref*})
> Logs a debug message, which includes the filename and line number of the calling routine.

## mod_perl–Specific Methods

The methods in this section do not have a counterpart in the C language API.

*$str* = *$r*->current_callback
> Returns the name of the current handler (e.g., PerlAuthz-Handler, PerlLogHandler, etc.).

*Apache*->exit([*$code*])
> Calls Perl's croak() to halt the script execution. If passed an argument of DONE, the child server process terminates once the current request has been processed.

$fh = Apache->gensym

    Generates an anonymous *glob* for use as a filehandle that is safe from namespace clashes.

$aref = $r->get_handlers($phase)

    Returns a reference to the list of subroutines registered to handle the specified request phase and configured to handle the current request.

Apache->httpd_conf($str)

    Evaluates Apache configuration directives contained in the multi-line string. Note that this method can be called only during server startup.

$bool = $r->module($module_name)

    Returns true if the specified Apache or Perl module has already been loaded ($module_name is taken to refer to an Apache module if its value ends with .c, otherwise a Perl module is assumed).

$bool = mod_perl::hook($name)

    Strips any prefix of Perl or suffix of Handler from the argument value and calls the Apache::perl_hook() method with the modified value.

$bool = Apache::perl_hook($name)

    Returns true if the specified callback hook is enabled (one of Access, Authen, Authz, ChildInit, Cleanup, Fixup, HeaderParser, Init, Log, Trans, or Type).

$r->post_connection($code_ref)

    Alias for the register_cleanup() method.

$r->push_handlers($phase => $code_ref)

    Adds the Perl handler routine, specified by $code_ref, to the current request's handler stack for the specified request phase.

$r = Apache->request([$r])

    Returns a reference to the current request object.

```
$r->set_handlers($phase => $aref)
```
> Sets the list of handlers for the specified request phase, specified as a reference to a list of subroutines. Specify undef to remove all handlers for the phase.

## The Apache::Server Class

The Apache::Server class provides methods to access information about the server configuration.

```
$s = $r->server
```
> Returns a reference to the server object.

```
$s = Apache->server
```
> Returns a reference to the server object.

```
$num = $s->gid
```
> Returns the numeric group ID under which the server answers requests. This is the value of the Apache Group directive.

```
$bool = $s->is_virtual
```
> Returns true if this is a virtual server.

```
$log = $s->log
```
> Returns a reference to an Apache::Log object.

```
$s->log_error($message)
```
> Logs an error message to the error log. This method is available in phases where there is no request object, such as during server startup.

```
$level = $s->loglevel
```
> Returns the current log level as specified by the LogLevel directive. Note that this method is added by the Apache::Log module, which must be explicitly loaded for the method to be recognized.

```
$aref = $s->names
```
> Returns a reference to a list of hostnames by which the current virtual host is known (as specified by Server-Alias directives).

`$s = $s->next`

Returns the next virtual server in the linked list of configured virtual hosts.

`$num = $s->port`

Returns the port number on which this server listens.

`$str = $s->server_admin`

Returns the email address set up with the ServerAdmin directive.

`$str = $s->server_hostname`

Returns the hostname used by this server.

`$num = $s->timeout([$newval])`

Gets or sets the value of the timeout (as set by the Timeout directive).

`$num = $s->uid`

Returns the numeric user ID under which the server answers requests. This is the value of the Apache User directive.

`$s->warn($message)`

Alias for Apache::warn(). This method is available in phases where there is no request object, such as during server startup.

## The Apache::Connection Class

The Apache::Connection class provides methods to access information about the current connection.

`$c = $r->connection`

Returns a connection object.

`$bool = $c->aborted`

Returns true if the client closed the connection.

`$str = $c->auth_type`

Returns the name of the authentication scheme that successfully authenticated $c->user, if any.

*$num = $c*->fileno([*$direction*])

> Returns the file descriptor of the output side of the connection, or the input side if *$direction* is specified explicitly as 0.

*$addr = $c*->local_addr

> Returns a packed SOCKADDR_IN address containing the port and address on the local host that the remote client is connected to.

*$addr = $c*->remote_addr([*$addr*])

> Gets or sets the port and address on the remote end of the connection as a packed SOCKADDR_IN structure.

*$str = $c*->remote_host

> Returns the name of the remote host if HostNameLookups is set to ON and the DNS lookup was successful; otherwise undef is returned.

*$str = $c*->remote_ip([*$ip*])

> Gets or sets the dotted decimal representation of the remote client's IP address.

*$str = $c*->remote_logname

> Returns the login name of the remote user if the IdentityCheck is set to ON and the information can be retrieved from the remote system; otherwise undef is returned.

*$str = $c*->user([*$username*])

> Gets or sets the authenticated username. This is set if an authentication check was successful. Note that *mod_perl* 1.25 adds a user() method to the Apache class and deprecates the use of the method in the Apache::Connection class, as this will ease migration to Apache 2.0.

## The Apache::Table Class

The Apache::Table class provides a tied interface to the Apache table data structures.

*$table = Apache::Table*->new(*$r*[, *$size*])
> Creates a new table object.

*$table*->add(*$key*, *$str_or_aref*)
> Adds a key/value pair to the table. Multiple values for a key are appended to a list. The value can be a string or an array reference.

*$table*->clear
> Empties the table.

*$table*->do(*$code_ref*)
> Iterates through the table, calling the subroutine passed as a code reference with each key/value pair in turn, and stopping if the subroutine returns a false value.

{*$str|@array*} = *$table*->get(*$key*)
> In a scalar context, returns the first value of the key; in an array context, returns all values of a multi-valued key.

*$table*->merge(*$key*, *$str_or_aref*)
> Merges multiple values for a key into a single comma-separated value.

*$table*->set(*$key*, *$str*)
> Sets the value for a key/value pair, replacing any previous values for the key.

*$table*->unset(*$key*)
> Removes a key and all associated values.

## The Apache::URI Class

The Apache::URI class provides methods for parsing and generating URIs.

*$uri* = Apache::URI->parse(*$r*[, *$string_uri*])
> Parses the URI into its components and returns a reference to an Apache::URI object. If a URI string is not specified, the URI of the current request is used. There are methods for getting and setting each of the components.

---

*$str* = *$uri*->fragment([*$str*])

    Gets or sets the fragment component of the URI.

*$str* = *$uri*->hostinfo([*$str*])

    Gets or sets the remote host information component of the URI. The general form is *username:password@hostname:port* for HTTP and FTP URIs.

*$str* = *$uri*->hostname([*$str*])

    Gets or sets the remote hostname component of the URI.

*$str* = *$uri*->password([*$str*])

    Gets or sets the password component of the URI.

*$str* = *$uri*->path([*$str*])

    Gets or sets the path component of the URI.

*$str* = *$uri*->path_info([*$str*])

    Gets or sets the additional path information component of the URI.

*$str* = *$uri*->port([*$str*])

    Gets or sets the port component of the URI.

*$str* = *$uri*->query([*$str*])

    Gets or sets the query string component of the URI.

*$str* = *$uri*->rpath

    Returns the *real path* part of the URI (the portion of the path component of the URI up to the path information part).

*$str* = *$uri*->scheme([*$str*])

    Gets or sets the scheme (protocol) component of the URI.

*$str* = *$uri*->user([*$str*])

    Gets or sets the username component of the URI.

*$str* = *$uri*->unparse

    Returns the string representation of the URI (without the additional path information). Relative URIs are resolved into absolute URIs.

## The Apache::Util Class

The `Apache::Util` class provides Perl interfaces to some utility functions written in C.

*$str* = Apache::Util::escape_html(*$html*)

Replaces all unsafe HTML characters (e.g., <, >, &, and ") with their entity representations. This helps in preventing exposure to cross-site scripting attacks.

*$str* = Apache::Util::escape_uri(*$uri*)

Replaces all unsafe characters with their URI-encoded escape sequences.

*$str* = Apache::Util::ht_time(*$time*[, *$fmt*[, *$GMT*]])

Formats a time value as a string by using the specified `strftime()`-style format or the default of "%d %b %Y %H:%M:%S %Z" (%Z is an Apache extension that expands to GMT). Ordinary characters in the format string are copied literally. Conversion specifiers are introduced by a percent sign (%) and are interpreted as follows:

| Spec. | Description |
|-------|-------------|
| %a | Abbreviated name of the day of the week |
| %A | Full name of the day of the week |
| %b | Abbreviated month name according to the current locale |
| %B | Full month name according to the current locale |
| %c | Preferred date and time representation for the current locale |
| %d | Two-digit day of the month (01–31) |
| %H | Two-digit hour using the 24-hour clock (00–23) |
| %I | Two-digit hour using the 12-hour clock (01–12) |
| %j | Three-digit day of the year (001–366) |
| %M | Two-digit minutes part of the time (00–59) |
| %m | Two-digit month number (01–12) |
| %p | Current locale's 12-hour clock A.M./P.M. indicator |

| Spec. | Description |
| --- | --- |
| %S | Seconds part of the time (00–61, to allow for leap seconds) |
| %U | Two-digit week number (00–53, where weeks start on a Sunday and week 1 is the first full week of the year) |
| %W | Two-digit week number (00–53, where weeks start on a Monday and week 1 is the first full week of the year) |
| %w | Day of the week (0–6, where 0 represents Sunday) |
| %X | Preferred time representation for the current locale (without the date) |
| %x | Preferred date representation for the current locale (without the time) |
| %Y | Year as a four-digit number (including the century) |
| %y | Year as a two-digit number (without the century) |
| %Z | Time zone abbreviation |

If a value of zero is passed for $GMT, the local time zone is used; otherwise the time is expressed in GMT.

$secs = Apache::Util::parsedate($date_str)

Converts a string representation of a date in HTTP or asctime() format into a Unix time value.

$str = Apache::Util::size_string($val)

Returns a string containing a formatted representation of a filesize value expressed in units of bytes, kilobytes, or megabytes, according to the magnitude of the value.

$str = Apache::Util::unescape_uri($uri)

Returns the URI string with all %XX hex escapes decoded.

$str = Apache::Util::unescape_uri_info($uri)

Returns the URI query string with all plus characters translated into spaces and all %XX hex escapes decoded.

$bool = Apache::Util::validate_password($raw, $enc)

Validates a plain text password against an encoded one and returns true if they match, false otherwise.

## The Apache::File Class

The Apache::File class provides methods for opening and manipulating files.

*$fh* = Apache::File->new([*$filename*])

Creates a new filehandle. If passed a filename, it is passed to the Perl open() function. Returns undef on failure.

*$fh*->open(*$filename*)

Passes the filename to the Perl open() function and associates the file with the filehandle object.

*$bool* = *$fh*->close

Closes the file open on the filehandle. The file is automatically closed when the filehandle goes out of scope, so it is often not necessary to make an explicit call to close().

{(*$filename*, *$fh*)|*$fh*} = Apache::File->tmpfile

Creates and opens a unique temporary file, which is deleted when the HTTP transaction is complete. Returns the name of the temporary file and either a filehandle open for reading (in a list context) or just the filehandle (in a scalar context).

The following methods are added to the Apache package.

*$r*->discard_request_body

Tests for the existence of a request body and, if present, discards it so that it is not read as the next request on a persistent connection. An error code is returned if the request is malformed.

*$r*->meets_conditions

Inspects the client HTTP headers that implement conditional GET and determines whether the rules are met. If the method returns anything other than OK, the handler should return with that value.

`$r->mtime`

> Returns the last modification time of the requested file as a Unix time value.

`$r->set_content_length([$length])`

> Sets the value of the Content-Length HTTP header. If no length is specified, the size of `$r->filename` is used.

`$r->set_etag`

> Sets the value of the ETag HTTP response header.

`$r->set_last_modified([$mtime])`

> Sets the value of the Last-Modified HTTP response header from the value returned by the mtime() method. If a time is supplied, update_mtime() is called to set the file's last modification time.

`$r->update_mtime([$mtime])`

> Updates the last modification time of the current request if the time specified is later than the current value. With no arguments, it uses the last modification time of `$r->filename`.

## Special Variables

Perl has numerous special variables, some of which behave differently in scripts running under *mod_perl*.

$0  Set to the filename of the script when running under Apache::Registry or Apache::PerlRun. Set to the path of the configuration file for code running inside a <Perl> section.

$^X  Path of the Apache binary.

$|  If true, causes Apache's output buffer to be flushed after each print().

$/  The Perl input record separator. Under *mod_perl*, it is reset back to the default value of newline after each request.

%@ A hash of error messages or exception values, keyed on the URI that generated the error.

%ENV

Contains the current environment. Variables specified with `PerlSetEnv` or `PerlPassEnv` are set up at the start of the request processing cycle. The normal CGI and SSI variables and variables specified with `SetEnv` or `PassEnv` are set up just before the content generation phase, unless `PerlSetupEnv` is set to `OFF`. The complete set of variables can be made available earlier in the request processing cycle by invoking the `setprocess_env()` method in a void context.

$ENV{MOD_PERL}

Set to true under *mod_perl*.

$ENV{GATEWAY_INTERFACE}

Set to `CGI-Perl/1.1` under *mod_perl*.

$ENV{PERL_SEND_HEADER}

Set to `ON` if `PerlSendHeader` is configured to be `ON`.

@INC

The Perl search path, which is the list of directories to be searched for scripts and modules evaluated with do *EXPR*, `require`, and `use`. The server root directory and its *lib/perl* subdirectory are appended to the default path. The array is reset after each request to the value it had at the end of server startup.

%INC

Hash containing entries for each file included via `do`, `require`, or `use`. The key is the filename requested and the value is the location of the file found. Once loading of a file has been noted in %INC, Perl does not attempt to load it again. The `Apache::StatINC` and `Apache::Reload` modules can be used to reload files that have changed.

`%SIG`
> Hash of signal handlers. Restored after each request to the state it was in at the end of server startup.

`$Apache::Server::AddPerlVersion`
> If true, the string `"Perl/$]"` is expanded and added to the `Server` HTTP header (the `$]` special variable holds the Perl version number).

`$Apache::Server::ConfigTestOnly`
> Set to true if the server is running in configuration test mode (i.e., the server was started with the `-t` command-line option).

`$Apache::Server::CWD`
> Set to the directory from which the server was started.

`$Apache::Server::Restarting`
> Set to nonzero in the parent server process when the server is restarted. The value is incremented each time the server is restarted.

`$Apache::Server::Starting`
> Set to 1 in the parent server process during startup.

`$Apache::Server::SaveConfig`
> Perl sections are compiled in the `Apache::ReadConfig` namespace. If this variable is set to true, the namespace is not flushed once the section has been processed, and configuration data from the section is available to Perl modules at request time.

`$Apache::Server::StrictPerlSections`
> If true, *mod_perl* aborts if a `<Perl>` section generates invalid Apache configuration syntax.

## The Apache::Constants Class

The `Apache::Contants` class provides access to all HTTP status codes as constant subroutines. By default, only those constants listed under the `:common` export tag are exported. Other groups of constants can be explicitly imported as required.

Note that explicitly importing only the required constants can save a considerable amount of memory.

:common

   The most commonly used constants: OK, DECLINED, DONE, NOT_FOUND, FORBIDDEN, AUTH_REQUIRED, and SERVER_ERROR.

:response

   Includes the :common response codes plus the following: DOCUMENT_FOLLOWS, MOVED, REDIRECT, USE_LOCAL_COPY, BAD_REQUEST, BAD_GATEWAY, RESPONSE_CODES, NOT_IMPLE-MENTED, CONTINUE, and NOT_AUTHORITATIVE.

:methods

   HTTP request method numbers: METHODS, M_GET, M_PUT, M_POST, M_DELET, M_CONNECT, M_OPTIONS, M_TRACE, M_PATCH, M_PROPFIND, M_PROPPATCH, M_MKCOL, M_COPY, M_MOVE, M_LOCK, M_UNLOCK, and M_INVALID.

:options

   Constants used with the allow_options() method: OPT_NONE, OPT_INDEXES, OPT_INCLUDES, OPT_SYM_LINKS, OPT_EXECCGI, OPT_UNSET, OPT_INCNOEXEC, OPT_SYM_OWNER, OPT_MULTI, and OPT_ALL.

:satisfy

   Constants used with the satisfy() method: SATISFY_ALL, SATISFY_ANY, and SATISFY_UNSPEC.

:remotehost

   Host lookup types used with get_remote_host() method: REMOTE_HOST, REMOTE_NAME, REMOTE_NOLOOKUP, and REMOTE_DOUBLE_REV.

:http

   Common HTTP response codes: HTTP_OK, HTTP_MOVED_TEMPORARILY, HTTP_MOVED_PERMANENTLY, HTTP_METHOD_NOT_ALLOWED, HTTP_NOT_MODIFIED, HTTP_UNAUTHORIZED, HTTP_FORBIDDEN, HTTP_NOT_FOUND, HTTP_BAD_REQUEST, HTTP_INTERNAL_SERVER_ERROR, HTTP_NOT_ACCEPTABLE, HTTP_NO_CONTENT, HTTP_PRECONDITION_FAILED, HTTP_SER-VICE_UNAVAILABLE, and HTTP_VARIANT_ALSO_VARIES.

---

:server

> Constants related to the version of Apache: MODULE_
> MAGIC_NUMBER, SERVER_VERSION, and SERVER_BUILT.

:config

> Constants used with configuration directive handlers:
> DECLINE_CMD.

:types

> Internal request types: DIR_MAGIC_TYPE.

:override

> Valid contexts for configuration directives: OR_NONE, OR_
> LIMIT, OR_OPTIONS, OR_FILEINFO, OR_AUTHCFG, OR_
> INDEXES, OR_UNSET, OR_ALL, ACCESS_CONF, and RSRC_CONF.

:args_how

> Constants that define configuration directive prototypes:
> RAW_ARGS, TAKE1, TAKE2, TAKE12, TAKE3, TAKE23, TAKE123,
> ITERATE, ITERATE2, FLAG, and NO_ARGS.

Other constants are defined but not included in the module's
@EXPORT or @EXPORT_OK arrays. Such constants can be accessed
using the fully qualified subroutine name, or the names may
be added to the @EXPORT_OK array in a server startup file and
then imported with use() where needed.

# mod_perl Configuration Directives

The Apache configuration directives specific to *mod_perl* are
described in a standard format, as shown here.

---

**DirectiveName**                                           GVSF*

DirectiveName *arg1 arg2*

Descriptive text.

---

The line after the directive name gives the syntax; the name of
the directive is given in bold type followed by its arguments.
Directive names are case-insensitive, as are most arguments
except those that refer to case-sensitive objects such as file-
names. The list of contexts in which the directive may be

---

used is given at the end of the line. This list can contain one or more of the following abbreviations:

G  Valid in global context (i.e., in the server configuration files outside of any virtual host or directory-type container)

V  Valid in a virtual host section

S  Valid in a directory-type section (<Directory>, <Files>, and <Location>)

F  Valid in a per-directory configuration file (named *.htaccess* by default)

\*  Indicates that the directive may be given more than once in a context

A description of the directive follows; the description includes the default value for the directive where appropriate.

The `Perl*Handler` directives install handler routines that are called for specified phases of the request-processing cycle. Apart from the child initialization and exit handlers, all handler routines are called with a reference to the request object as the sole argument. Note that not all handlers may be available depending on how *mod_perl* was compiled.

A handler may be specified as an anonymous subroutine, a subroutine name qualified with a package name, or just a package name, in which case the subroutine name defaults to `handler`. If the handler is specified as a package name, it may be prefixed with a plus sign (+), which instructs *mod_perl* to preload the handler module at server startup.

---

**<Perl>**                                                        GVSF\*

```
<Perl> # Perl code </Perl>
```

Container section for embedding Perl code in Apache configuration files; it can contain any Perl code, which is evaluated in the `Apache::ReadConfig` package as the configuration files are processed. Having evaluated the code, *mod_perl* examines the package's symbol table for any variables that match the names of Apache directives, and

---

passes the names and values through Apache's normal configuration mechanism. The type of variable to use depends on the directive:

*Directives taking no arguments*
 Assign the empty string to a scalar variable

*Directives taking one argument*
 Assign the value to a scalar variable

*Directives taking multiple arguments*
 Assign the values as a list to an array variable

Container sections are represented by Perl hashes with the argument as the hash key. Sections with multiple same-value keys are represented as arrays of references to the individual hashes. Nested sections are represented as nested hashes. For example:

```
<Perl>
    use Apache::Registry;
    $SSLEnable   = '';
    $DefaultType = 'text/plain';
    @AddType     = ( 'images/jpeg' => 'jpg', 'jpeg' );

    $Location{'/perl'} = {
        SetHandler  => 'perl-script',
        PerlHandler => 'Apache::Registry'
    };
</Perl>
```

The contents of the $PerlConfig variable and the @PerlConfig array are treated as raw Apache configuration data, and their values are fed directly to the Apache configuration engine.

Perl sections are available only if *mod_perl* was built with the PERL_SECTIONS configuration variable set.

---

**PerlAccessHandler**                                    GVSF*

PerlAccessHandler *handler* ...

Installs one or more handlers for the access control phase (available only if *mod_perl* was built with the PERL_ACCESS configuration variable set).

---

## PerlAddVar GVSF*

PerlAddVar *name value*

Sets the value of a Perl configuration variable, which can then be accessed within handlers via the dir_config() method. If the variable already exists, a further value is added, making the variable multi-valued.

## PerlAuthenHandler GVSF*

PerlAuthenHandler *handler* ...

Installs one or more handlers for the authentication phase, which should check the supplied credentials (available only if *mod_perl* was built with the PERL_AUTHEN configuration variable set).

## PerlAuthzHandler GVSF*

PerlAuthzHandler *handler* ...

Installs one or more handlers for the authorization phase, which should determine whether an authenticated user is allowed access to the resource (available only if *mod_perl* was built with the PERL_AUTHZ configuration variable set).

## PerlChildInitHandler GV*

PerlChildInitHandler *handler* ...

Installs one or more handlers that are called immediately after a child server process is spawned (available only if *mod_perl* was built with the PERL_CHILD_INIT configuration variable set).

## PerlChildExitHandler

PerlChildExitHandler *handler* ...

Installs one or more handlers that are called just before the child server process exits (available only if *mod_perl* was built with the PERL_CHILD_EXIT configuration variable set).

### PerlCleanupHandler
GVSF*

`PerlCleanupHandler` *handler* ...

Installs one or more handlers for the cleanup phase (available only if *mod_perl* was built with the `PERL_CLEANUP` configuration variable set).

### PerlDispatchHandler
GVSF

`PerlDispatchHandler` *subroutine-name*

Specifies a subroutine to handle loading and invoking handlers in place of *mod_perl*'s normal mechanism (available only if *mod_perl* was built with the `PERL_DISPATCH` configuration variable set). The routine is passed a request object and the name of the handler (or a code reference to it) that would normally be invoked to process the phase.

### PerlFixupHandler
GVSF*

`PerlFixupHandler` *handler* ...

Installs one or more handlers for the fixup phase (available only if *mod_perl* was built with the `PERL_FIXUP` configuration variable set).

### PerlFreshRestart
GV

`PerlFreshRestart` { ON|OFF }

If set to ON, *mod_perl* reloads all loaded Perl modules whenever the server is restarted. The default is OFF.

### PerlHandler
GVSF*

`PerlHandler` *handler* ...

Installs one or more handlers for the content generation phase. For example:

```
<Location /perl-bin>
    SetHandler  perl-script
    PerlHandler Apache::OutputChain  \
                Apache::GzipChain    \
                Apache::PassFile
</Location>
```

In contrast to handlers for other phases, Perl content handlers must be explicitly specified as perl-script with the SetHandler directive.

### PerlHeaderParserHandler
GVSF*

PerlHeaderParserHandler *handler* ...

Installs one or more handlers that are called just before the content generation phase (available only if *mod_perl* was built with the PERL_HEADER_PARSER configuration variable set).

### PerlInitHandler
GVSF*

PerlInitHandler *handler* ...

This is an alias for the first relevant handler. <Directory>, <Location>, and <Files> sections can be applied only after the URI has been translated, so within these sections the directive is an alias for the PerlHeaderParserHandler directive. If used outside these sections, it is an alias for the PerlPostReadRequestHandler directive. (Available only if *mod_perl* was built with the PERL_INIT configuration variable set.)

### PerlLogHandler
GVSF*

PerlLogHandler *handler* ...

Installs a handler for the logging phase (available only if *mod_perl* was built with the PERL_LOG configuration variable set).

### PerlModule
GVSF*

PerlModule *module* ...

Loads the specified Perl modules at server startup. Perl searches the @INC path for *.pm* files that match each of the modules.

### PerlPassEnv
GV*

PerlPassEnv *name* ...

Passes a value from the environment to the corresponding %ENV element at the start of the request cycle.

### PerlPostReadRequestHandler
GV*

PerlPostReadRequestHandler *handler* ...

Installs a handler that is called after a request has been received and the header fields parsed, but before the URI has been translated

---

(available only if *mod_perl* was built with the configuration variable `PERL_POST_READ_REQUEST` set).

## PerlRequire                                                    GVSF*

`PerlRequire` *script-path* ...

Loads the specified scripts at server startup.

## PerlRestartHandler                                             GV*

`PerlRestartHandler` *handler* ...

Specifies a routine to be called in the main server process when the server is restarted (available only if *mod_perl* was built with the `PERL_RESTART` configuration variable set).

## PerlSendHeader                                                 GVSF

`PerlSendHeader` { ON|OFF }

If set to `ON`, all text sent to the client up to the first blank line is passed to the `send_cgi_header()` method. The default value is `OFF`.

## PerlSetEnv                                                     GVSF*

`PerlSetEnv` *name value*

Sets the environment variable at the start of the request cycle, or during server startup if the directive appears outside of a `<Directory>`, `<Location>`, or `<Files>` section.

## PerlSetupEnv                                                   GVSF

`PerlSetupEnv` { ON|OFF }

Controls whether *mod_perl* sets up the `%ENV` hash. The default is `ON`, and the hash is normally filled in just before the content generation phase. Environment variables specified with `PerlPassEnv` and `PerlSetEnv` are set up at the start of the request processing cycle.

## PerlSetVar                                                     GVSF*

`PerlSetVar` *name value*

Sets the value of a Perl configuration variable, which can then be accessed within handlers via the `dir_config()` method. If the variable already exists, its value is replaced.

## PerlTaintCheck                                                    GV

```
PerlTaintCheck  { ON|OFF }
```

If set to ON, Perl's taint checks are enabled (equivalent to Perl's -T
option). Taint checks prevent Perl code from inadvertently and inse-
curely using data that originated outside the program. The checks can
be enabled only for *mod_perl* as a whole, not for individual scripts.
By default, taint checks are disabled (OFF).

## PerlTransHandler                                                  GV*

```
PerlTransHandler  handler ...
```

Installs a handler for the URI translation phase, which should take a
partial URI and transform it (available only if *mod_perl* was built with
the PERL_TRANS configuration variable set). The transformation can
result in a filename, a change to the request, or the installation of new
handlers based on the URI.

## PerlTypeHandler                                                   GVSF*

```
PerlTypeHandler  handler ...
```

Installs a handler for the type checking phase (available only if *mod_
perl* was built with the PERL_TYPE configuration variable set).

## PerlWarn                                                          GV

```
PerlWarn  { ON|OFF }
```

If set to ON, Perl warnings are enabled for all Perl code within the
server. Warnings can be enabled for individual scripts by including
the -w switch on the #! line. The default value is OFF.

# Apache/Perl Modules

Many Apache/Perl modules have been written and made
available on CPAN, the Comprehensive Perl Archive Network
(*http://www.cpan.org*). The  *http://search.cpan.org* web  site
and the CPAN module provide search facilities for CPAN.

This section contains lists of modules grouped by functionality. It is a brief snapshot of the modules on CPAN written

---

specifically for use with *mod_perl*. Since the modules on CPAN are continuously changing, you should check there for definitive information on any module that you want to use in your applications.

Modules that are included in the *mod_perl* distribution (which is itself on CPAN) are identified with a filled star (★) for core modules and an outline star (☆) for non-core modules. Core modules are those Perl classes that are built into the *mod_perl* Apache module.

## Template Systems and Frameworks

There are many modules that provide frameworks for embedding Perl code within web documents. The most popular are Apache::ASP, Apache::Embperl, and Apache::Mason—these three as well as all the others are described here.

Apache::AO
> A servlet engine for Perl that provides session tracking and persistence, authentication and authorization, simple configuration, and customizable logging.

Apache::ASP
> An implementation of Active Server Pages (ASP) that uses Perl as the scripting language. See the web site *http://www.apache-asp.org*.

Apache::CIPP
> Apache/Perl module for CIPP (CGI Perl Preprocessor).

Apache::Dispatch
> Translates URIs into class and method names and runs them as Perl handlers.

Apache::Embperl
> A processor for embedding Perl code within HTML pages, providing meta-commands for conditional and loop constructs, automatic generation of HTML tables and lists from Perl arrays or function calls (including data fetched from databases with DBI), and persistent session management. See *http://perl.apache.org/embperl/*.

`Apache::EmbperlChain`

Calls `HTML::Embperl` to process output from other Perl handlers.

`Apache::EP`

Another system for embedding Perl into HTML. Provides facilities for localization, database access, sending email, etc.

`Apache::ePerl`

One of the first HTML template systems. See the web site at *http://www.engelschall.com/sw/eperl/*.

`Apache::HeavyCGI`

Framework to run complex CGI tasks on an Apache server.

`Apache::HTPL`

Hyper Text Programming Language: a Perl-based scripting tool for creating web content.

`Apache::Include` ☆

Allows `Apache::Registry` scripts to be invoked from within Server-Side Includes.

`Apache::iNcom`

An e-commerce framework providing session management, shopping cart management, input validation, order management, user management, easy database access, internationalization, and error handling.

`Apache::Mason`

A Perl-based web site development and delivery system that allows web pages to be built from components. See *http://www.masonhq.com*.

`Apache::mod_pml`

PML Markup Language: a text preprocessor with support for variables, flow control, and macros.

`Apache::OWA`

Runs Oracle PL/SQL Web Toolkit applications.

Apache::PageKit

An application framework that uses HTML::Template and XML to separate web page design from content. It includes session management, authentication, form validation, co-branding, and a content management system. See *http://pagekit.org*.

Apache::SimpleReplace

A simple template framework that inserts the contents of the HTML files being served into a specified template in place of a single marker string.

Apache::SSI

Perl implementation of Server-Side Includes.

Apache::Taco

A template-driven application framework for dynamic content.

Apache::Template

An Apache interface to the Template Toolkit: a fast, flexible, and extensible template-processing framework.

Apache::UploadSvr

A small web publishing system that includes authentication, simple security, preview, directory viewer, and an interface to delete files.

AxKit

An XML delivery toolkit for Apache. See *http://axkit.org*.

## Content Generation

Apache::Album

A virtual photo album with on-the-fly generation of thumbnail images and configurable layout.

Apache::Archive

Serves indexes of *.tar* and *.tar.gz* archive files and individual files extracted from those files.

`Apache::AutoIndex`
> A subclassable directory indexer module.

`Apache::Compress`
> Compresses the output from other Perl handlers on the fly for user agents that understand the *gzip* encoding.

`Apache::Filter`
> Provides a framework for filtering the output of previous content handlers.

`Apache::Gateway`
> A multiplexing gateway.

`Apache::GD::Graph`
> Generates and returns a PNG format graph based on the arguments supplied in the query string.

`Apache::GzipChain`
> Compresses the output from other Perl handlers on the fly for user agents that understand the *gzip* encoding.

`Apache::Layer`
> Layers multiple content trees on top of each other.

`Apache::Motd`
> Displays a message of the day.

`Apache::MP3`
> Generates playlists from directory hierarchies containing MP3 files.

`Apache::OutputChain`
> Provides a mechanism for chaining Perl content handlers.

`Apache::PassFile`
> Copies the file, resulting in URI-to-filename translation to `STDOUT`. This module is useful as part of an output chain.

`Apache::PerlRun` ☆
> A single-shot CGI emulator.

`Apache::PrettyPerl`
> Dynamically pretty-prints Perl source code as HTML pages.

Apache::PrettyText
Dynamically formats plain text files.

Apache::Registry ☆
A CGI emulator.

Apache::Sandwich
Adds headers and footers to HTML documents on the fly.

Apache::SetWWWTheme
Creates a standard header, footer, and sidebar for HTML pages and allows <BODY> element attributes to be over-ridden to provide a consistent look and feel to a web site.

Apache::Stage
Implements staging directories.

## Access Controls

Access controls include authentication (checking whether the credentials supplied, normally a username and password, are valid) and authorization (checking whether the authenticated user is permitted to access the requested resource). Note, however, that HTTP basic authentication over a non-SSL connection is inherently insecure; it is therefore recommended that password files or databases used for system access are not used with this method of web authentication. Authentication information can be stored in many different ways, and there is a correspondingly large array of modules to use that information.

Apache::AuthCookie
Intercepts a user's first unauthenticated access to protected documents and stores a session key as a cookie to be presented on subsequent requests. Requests with a valid session key are deemed to be authenticated. Apache::AuthCookie is a base class and does not itself implement any authentication mechanism.

`Apache::AuthCookieDBI`
> A ticket-issuing authentication and authorization system using a DBI database (a subclass of `Apache::Auth-Cookie`).

`Apache::AuthDBI`
> Performs authentication and authorization against a database accessed through the Perl DBI.

`Apache::AuthLDAP`
> Authenticates against an LDAP database.

`Apache::AuthNetLDAP`
> Authenticates users via LDAP by using the `Net::LDAP` module.

`Apache::AuthPerLDAP`
> Provides basic authentication against an LDAP server using Netscape's PerLDAP toolkit.

`Apache::AuthTicket`
> Provides ticket-based access control using HTTP cookies to check if a user is authorized to view a page. `Apache::AuthCookie` is used as the underlying mechanism for managing cookies.

`Apache::AuthenCache`
> Caches the results of authentication lookups on a per-process basis.

`Apache::AuthenIMAP`
> Authenticates against an IMAP server.

`Apache::AuthenNIS`
> Authenticates against NIS.

`Apache::AuthenN2`
> Authenticates against NT and NIS+ servers.

`Apache::AuthenNISPlus`
> Authenticates against an NIS+ server.

`Apache::AuthenPasswd`
Authenticates against the system password file.

`Apache::AuthenPasswdSvr`
Passes user credentials to a password server for checking.

`Apache::AuthenRadius`
Authenticates against a RADIUS server.

`Apache::AuthenSmb`
Authenticates against an SMB server.

`Apache::AuthenURL`
Authenticates via a request to a remote HTTP server that supports basic authentication, supplying the original credentials with that request for authentication.

`Apache::AuthzNetLDAP`
Performs authorization checks against an LDAP database.

`Apache::AuthzNIS`
Performs authorization checks against an NIS database.

`Apache::AuthzPasswd`
Performs authorization checks against an *htgroup* file.

`Apache::DBILogin`
Authenticates against a relational database by trying to connect with the supplied credentials, rather than checking the credentials against information stored in the database.

`Apache::PHLogin`
Authenticates against a PH database.

`Apache::RefererBlock`
Redirects or denies access to configured resources based on the MIME type of the resource and the value of the `Referer` header in the HTTP request.

# URI Translation

Apache::Backhand

Integrates *mod_perl* with the *mod_backhand* Apache module, which implements load-balancing between a cluster of Apache servers.

Apache::Proxy

A Perl interface to the *mod_proxy* Apache module.

Apache::ProxyPass

Implements the functionality of the *mod_proxy* Apache module in Perl (based on Apache::ProxyPassThru).

Apache::ProxyPassThru

A basic proxy module that also works with Apache::DumpHeaders to log headers from the remote site.

Apache::ProxyStuff

Adds headers and footers to HTML content proxied from other web servers.

Apache::RandomLocation

Generates redirects for configured locations to a destination picked randomly from a list.

Apache::RedirectDBI

Redirects requests to one of a list of specified directories if the authenticated username is present in a corresponding database table.

Apache::ReverseProxy

A reverse proxy module that is intended to replace Apache::ProxyPass.

Apache::RewritingProxy

A rewriting proxy that parses HTML documents and adjusts any links it finds that refer to the proxied site.

Apache::TimedRedirect

> Generates redirects for requests occurring within a specified time period.

Apache::TransLDAP

> Translates requests for configured user directories by mapping to LDAP database entries.

## Logging

Apache::DBILogConfig

> Logs request information as specified by a format string in an SQL database using Perl DBI.

Apache::DBILogger

> Logs request information in a fixed table in an SQL database.

Apache::LogFile

> An interface to Apache's logging routines.

Apache::Traffic

> Tracks the total number of hits and bytes transferred per day on a per-user basis. The information is held in a shared memory segment, and can be viewed with the script provided or with a custom script that you write yourself.

Apache::UserTrack

> Implements the functionality of the *mod_usertrack* Apache module in Perl.

## Low-Level Interfaces

Apache ★

> The Perl interface to the Apache server API.

Apache::Connection ★

> Provides details of the network connection to the client.

`Apache::Constants` ★

The constants defined in Apache header files.

`Apache::Cookie`

A cookie-handling module based on Lincoln Stein's `CGI::Cookie` module. This module is part of the *libapreq* package.

`Apache::File` ★

Fast object-oriented functions for manipulating files on the server.

`Apache::Icon`

Provides an interface for looking up icon images.

`Apache::Log` ★

The interface to Apache logging methods.

`Apache::Module`

Provides an interface to the list of Apache modules configured in the server, with their module, command, and handler data structures.

`Apache::ModuleConfig` ★

The interface to Apache's module configuration mechanism.

`Apache::Options` ☆

Exports `OPT_*` constants.

`Apache::PerlSections` ☆

Provides two public functions, `dump()` and `store()`, to dump and save the contents of `<Perl>` configuration sections, respectively.

`Apache::ReadConfig` ★

The namespace used by `<Perl>` configuration sections to store global variables.

`Apache::Request`

A subclass of the `Apache` class that adds methods for parsing `GET` and `POST` requests. This module is part of the *libapreq* package.

---

Apache::Scoreboard
    A Perl interface to Apache's scoreboard.

Apache::ScoreboardGraph
    Generates a graphical representation of the Apache score-
    board.

Apache::Server ★
    Provides access to information about the server configu-
    ration.

Apache::SubProcess
    Perl interface to the Apache subprocess API.

Apache::SubRequest ★
    The lookup_uri() and lookup_file() methods return an
    object of this class, a subclass of the Apache class that
    adds a single method to run the content generation phase
    for the subrequest.

Apache::Symbol ☆
    Enables subroutines eligible for inlining to be undefined
    to avoid warnings on server restart.

Apache::Table ★
    The interface to the Apache table data structures.

Apache::URI ★
    Methods for parsing and recombining URI components.

Apache::Util ★
    Perl interfaces to various Apache C utility functions.

mod_perl ★
    Provides methods to determine the version of *mod_perl*
    and which features are supported.

## Development, Debugging, and Monitoring

Apache::DB
    Allows the Perl interactive debugger to be used on an
    Apache/*mod_perl* server process.

`Apache::Debug` ☆

    Utilities for debugging embedded Perl code.

`Apache::DebugInfo`

    Enables logging of per-request information based on IP address or file type.

`Apache::DProf`

    Runs a `Devel::DProf` profiler inside each child server process.

`Apache::DumpHeaders`

    Dumps HTTP headers of requests. Can be configured to dump requests from specified IP addresses, and can also be triggered by another module.

`Apache::ExtUtils` ☆

    Utilities for generating XSUB code for Perl modules that define their own Apache configuration directives. These are defined by static C structures that cannot be built dynamically at runtime.

`Apache::FakeRequest` ☆

    Implements a fake request object that is useful for debugging *mod_perl* scripts.

`Apache::httpd_conf` ☆

    Generates *httpd.conf* files for configuring Apache when testing *mod_perl* modules and scripts.

`Apache::GTopLimit`

    Kills off Apache child server processes if they grow too large or if the amount of shared memory drops below a specified limit.

`Apache::Leak` ☆

    A tool for tracking memory leaks in *mod_perl* code.

`Apache::Peek`

    A tool for examining raw Perl datatypes.

Apache::PerlVINC

Allows different versions of Perl modules to be used in different virtual hosts.

Apache::RegistryLexInfo

Takes snapshots of the internal Perl data structures that are used to store lexical variables before and after an Apache::Registry script is run, and prints any differences. This may not be suitable reading for the faint of heart.

Apache::Reload

Reloads modules that have changed; can be configured to check and reload only specified modules or modules that use this module.

Apache::ShowRequest

Runs a request exactly as Apache would, using the given path information as the URI and printing information about the phases that are invoked.

Apache::SizeLimit ☆

Kills off Apache child server processes if they grow too large.

Apache::SmallProf

Hooks Devel::SmallProf, a line-by-line code profiler, into *mod_perl*.

Apache::src ☆

Provides methods for locating and parsing components of the Apache source code.

Apache::StatINC ☆

Checks the Perl search path (@INC) on every request for modules that have changed, and reloads them.

Apache::Status ☆

Provides dynamic status and debug information about the *mod_perl* interpreter.

`Apache::Symdump` ☆
> Uses `Devel::Symdump` to record snapshots of the symbol table of the embedded Perl interpreter.

`Apache::test` ☆
> Provides utility functions for use in module test scripts.

`Apache::VMonitor`
> A visual system and Apache server monitor that can report on processes, mounted filesystems, disk usage, and network interface status.

`Apache::Watchdog::RunAway`
> A watchdog system for monitoring Apache child server processes that are hanging.

## Miscellaneous

`Apache::DBI`
> Keeps DBI database connections persistent on a per-process basis.

`Apache::Keywords`
> Maintains counts of keywords as a personal profile in a cookie. The supplied handler method counts the occurrences of keywords in <META> elements in static HTML documents served and is intended to be configured as a fixup handler.

`Apache::Htgroup`
> Manages Apache *htgroup* files.

`Apache::Htpasswd`
> Manages Apache *htaccess* password files.

`Apache::Language`
> Provides support for message strings in multiple languages.

`Apache::MimeXML`
> Detects the encoding of XML files.

---

Apache::Mmap

Maps files into the address space of the server using the mmap() system call.

Apache::Mysql

An older persistent database module for MySQL. This module is superseded by Apache::DBI, which should be used instead.

Apache::RegistryLoader ☆

Precompiles Apache::Registry scripts at server startup.

Apache::RequestNotes

Provides a simple interface allowing all phases of the request cycle access to cookie or form input parameters in a consistent manner.

Apache::Resource ☆

Sets resource limits on Apache server child processes.

Apache::Roaming

Implements a Netscape Roaming Access server, which allows Netscape Communicator clients to store their profiles centrally.

Apache::Session

A persistent session storage manager.

Apache::SIG ☆

Enables Apache's signal handlers to be overridden with Perl's.

Apache::Sybase::CTlib

Provides an interface to Sybase database servers and maintains persistent connections.

Apache::TempFile

Generates names for temporary files, which are automatically removed when the current request has been completed.

```
Apache::Throttle
```
Negotiates content based on the speed of the connection. Includes a script to generate images of different sizes.

# CGI Environment Variables

When Apache is running with *mod_perl*, it sets up the following CGI environment variables for content generation handlers (unless the `PerlSetupEnv` directive is specified as `OFF`). Variables not defined by the CGI specification are marked with a diamond (♦). Note that HTTP request header field values are added to the environment with the prefix `HTTP_`, and any hyphens in the header field name are changed to underscores.

```
AUTH_TYPE
```
Authentication method used (if subject to authentication).

```
CONTENT_LENGTH
```
Length of entity body (e.g., for `POST` requests).

```
CONTENT_TYPE
```
MIME type of entity body (e.g., for `POST` requests).

```
DOCUMENT_ROOT ♦
```
Value of the `DocumentRoot` directive.

```
GATEWAY_INTERFACE
```
CGI version; in a normal CGI environment this is set to `CGI/1.1`, but under *mod_perl* it is set to `CGI-Perl/1.1`.

```
PATH_INFO
```
URI part after script identifier.

```
PATH_TRANSLATED
```
`PATH_INFO` translated for the filesystem.

```
QUERY_STRING
```
Query string from URI (if present).

REMOTE_ADDR
> IP address of client.

REMOTE_HOST
> DNS name of client (if resolved).

REMOTE_IDENT
> Remote user ID (unreliable, even if available).

REMOTE_USER
> Name of the authenticated user (if request is subject to authentication).

REQUEST_METHOD
> HTTP request method.

SCRIPT_NAME
> Virtual path of the script.

SERVER_ADMIN ◆
> Value of the ServerAdmin directive.

SERVER_ADDR
> IP address of the server.

SERVER_NAME
> Hostname of the server.

SERVER_PORT
> Port number of the server.

SERVER_PROTOCOL
> Name and version of the protocol.

SERVER_SOFTWARE
> Server software name and version.

UNIQUE_ID ◆
> A token that is unique across all requests (only if the *mod_unique_id* Apache module is active).

# HTTP Status Codes

The following table lists the HTTP status codes, along with the symbolic names used in the Apache source code and in *mod_perl*. The Apache::Constants class exports a subset of these symbols with the :http export tag; others can be explicitly imported.

The numeric status code values are defined in RFC 2616. See the *HTTP Pocket Reference* for a detailed summary of the status codes.

| Code | Name |
|------|------|
| 100 | HTTP_CONTINUE |
| 101 | HTTP_SWITCHING_PROTOCOLS |
| 200 | HTTP_OK |
| 201 | HTTP_CREATED |
| 202 | HTTP_ACCEPTED |
| 203 | HTTP_NON_AUTHORITATIVE |
| 204 | HTTP_NO_CONTENT |
| 205 | HTTP_RESET_CONTENT |
| 206 | HTTP_PARTIAL_CONTENT |
| 300 | HTTP_MULTIPLE_CHOICES |
| 301 | HTTP_MOVED_PERMANENTLY |
| 302 | HTTP_MOVED_TEMPORARILY |
| 303 | HTTP_SEE_OTHER |
| 304 | HTTP_NOT_MODIFIED |
| 305 | HTTP_USE_PROXY |
| 400 | HTTP_BAD_REQUEST |
| 401 | HTTP_UNAUTHORIZED |
| 402 | HTTP_PAYMENT_REQUIRED |
| 403 | HTTP_FORBIDDEN |
| 404 | HTTP_NOT_FOUND |
| 405 | HTTP_METHOD_NOT_ALLOWED |
| 406 | HTTP_NOT_ACCEPTABLE |

| Code | Name |
|------|------|
| 407 | HTTP_PROXY_AUTHENTICATION_REQUIRED |
| 408 | HTTP_REQUEST_TIMEOUT |
| 409 | HTTP_CONFLICT |
| 410 | HTTP_GONE |
| 411 | HTTP_LENGTH_REQUIRED |
| 412 | HTTP_PRECONDITION_FAILED |
| 413 | HTTP_REQUEST_ENTITY_TOO_LARGE |
| 414 | HTTP_REQUEST_URI_TOO_LARGE |
| 415 | HTTP_UNSUPPORTED_MEDIA_TYPE |
| 500 | HTTP_INTERNAL_SERVER_ERROR |
| 501 | HTTP_NOT_IMPLEMENTED |
| 502 | HTTP_BAD_GATEWAY |
| 503 | HTTP_SERVICE_UNAVAILABLE |
| 504 | HTTP_GATEWAY_TIME_OUT |
| 505 | HTTP_VERSION_NOT_SUPPORTED |
| 506 | HTTP_VARIANT_ALSO_VARIES |

# HTTP Header Fields

HTTP header fields are defined in RFC 2616. They are categorized as follows:

*Request header fields*
Contain additional information about the request

*Response header fields*
Contain additional information about the response

*General header fields*
Applicable to both request and response messages

*Entity header fields*
Contain information about the entity body or the resource identified by the request

The following table summarizes the HTTP header fields; see the *HTTP Pocket Reference* for more details.

| Syntax | Category |
| --- | --- |
| Accept: *media-types*[;q=*qvalue*][, ...] | Request |
| Accept-Charset: *charset*[;q=*qvalue*][, ...] | Request |
| Accept-Encoding: *encoding*[;q=*qvalue*][, ...] | Request |
| Accept-Language: *lang*[;q=*qvalue*][, ...] | Request |
| Accept-Ranges:{bytes\|none} | Response |
| Age: *seconds* | Response |
| Allow: *method*[, ...] | Entity |
| Authorization: *scheme credentials* | Request |
| Cache-Control: *directive* | General |
| Connection: close | General |
| Content-Base: *uri* | Entity |
| Content-Encoding: *enc* | Entity |
| Content-Language: *lang* | Entity |
| Content-Length: *len* | Entity |
| Content-MD5: *digest* | Entity |
| Content-Range: bytes *range/length* | Entity |
| Content-Type: *media-type* | Entity |
| Cookie: *name=value*[; ...] | Request |
| Date: *date* | General |
| ETag: *entity-tag* | Response |
| Expect: *expectation* | Request |
| Expires: *date* | Entity |
| From: *email-address* | Request |
| Host: *hostname*[:*port*] | Request |
| If-Match: *entity-tag* | Request |
| If-Modified-Since: *date* | Request |
| If-None-Match: *entity-tag* | Request |
| If-Range: {*entity tag\|date*} | Request |
| If-Unmodified-Since: *date* | Request |
| Last-Modified: *date* | Entity |

| Syntax | Category |
|---|---|
| Location: *uri* | Response |
| Max-Forwards: *number* | Request |
| MIME-Version: *version* | General |
| Pragma: {no-cache\|*extension-pragma*} | General |
| Proxy-Authenticate: *challenge* | Response |
| Proxy-Authorization: *credentials* | Request |
| Public: *method*... | Response |
| Range: bytes=*n*[-*m*][, ...] | Request |
| Referer: *url* | Request |
| Retry-After: {*date*\|*seconds*} | Response |
| Server: *string* | Response |
| Set-Cookie: *name*=*value*[; *options*] | Response |
| TE: *coding* | Request |
| Trailer: *header* | General |
| Transfer-Encoding: *coding* | General |
| Upgrade: *protocol*[, ...] | General |
| User-Agent: *string* | Request |
| Vary: *header*[, ...] | Response |
| Via: [*protocol*/]*version* [(*comment*)] [, ...] | General |
| Warning: *code agent* "*text*" [*date*] | General |
| WWW-Authenticate: *scheme realm* | Response |

# Index of Modules

# Index of Methods

# Web Programming